# Three Years in a Colombian Prison: My Life in La Picota as Told to Marnie Gellhorn

Marnie Gellhorn

Published by AL Press, 2024.

While every precaution has been taken in the preparation of this book, the publisher assumes no responsibility for errors or omissions, or for damages resulting from the use of the information contained herein.

THREE YEARS IN A COLOMBIAN PRISON: MY LIFE IN LA PICOTA AS TOLD TO MARNIE GELLHORN

**First edition. December 28, 2024.**

Copyright © 2024 Marnie Gellhorn.

ISBN: 979-8230477358

Written by Marnie Gellhorn.

# Table of Contents

*To the families of Aristides and every other incarcerated individual. Your sacrifices and your pain is not forgotten.*

"One of the many lessons that one learns in prison is, that things are what they are and will be what they will be."

Oscar Wilde


"Prisons do not disappear social problems, they disappear human beings. Homelessness, unemployment, drug addiction, mental illness, and illiteracy are only a few of the problems that disappear from public view when the human beings contending with them are relegated to cages."

Angela Davis

# Author's note

This book is a collaboration between Aristides Jesus Gonzalez Riohacha and myself. Much of this book is a direct translation based on multiple interviews with Mr. Gonzalez Riohacha as he shared his story with me. I have taken the liberty, at times, to add my perspectives and some background for readers who may be unfamiliar with Colombia, Colombian history and culture.

I first met Aristides as a result of a strange twist of fate. An old friend from college contacted me, stating, "You need to come down here and hear this story." This is not as rare as it sounds in my line of work. As a freelance journalist, specializing in international news and events, I frequently get these sorts of calls. But I have never been called to Colombia before. Usually, my work takes me to Iran, Iraq or Afghanistan. I've been to Pakistan, Syria and Lebanon. I've even been called to Kuwait, Saudia Arabia and Qatar a couple of times, especially after my husband died. I've also done several series based in my adopted hometown of Memphis, Tennessee. But I've never been called to South America before, so I was intrigued, to say the least.

It turns out, my old friend, Katie had semi-retired to Colombia where she met the family of Aristides, quite by accident, while riding on the bus one day. She became close friends with Monica Camille Toussaint, who shared the story of her husband with her. When Aristides was released on probational house arrest,

## 2

Katie immediately called me to come interview him in person. I only hesitated for a few minutes, I mean, what do I know about prison? I know a lot about war, and the suffering that goes along with it. But this was an entirely new experience for me, and I wanted to share it with you.

It was challenging to work with Aristides to translate his words and his experiences into a cohesive story that the average American reader can understand.

I hope that Aristides story resonates with you, like it did with me.

Some people will question how the story of a former inmate in the Colombian justice system can have anything in common with their life back home in Memphis, Los Angeles, Florida or the heartland of the United States. But they shouldn't.

We can all acknowledge that our (American) justice system remains rife with privilege and advantages for the rich, with disproportionate sentences, harsh punishments and implicit biases against minorities and the poor, but we don't seem to have the will to do anything about it. If anything, American society becomes more like "La Miserable" every year. More and more of us sink into poverty and despair, becoming like Jean Valjean and Fantine every day, as our elected officials advise us to eat cake. They argue over trivialities like how many angels can dance of the head of a pin as millions of us go without health care, adequate pensions or any sort of safety net. The situation is even more dire if you've been marked with the scarlet "C" for convict, even after you've served your time.

There are few Myriels to show us the compassion our society desperately needs. I am not suggesting that we "go easy" on career criminals or ignore the rules of society, only that we not forget, that these individuals, our Aristides have their place in society too. We should also acknowledge that this affects a lot of individuals and their families.

With over 2 million people incarcerated in the United States, there is a pretty good chance that you, or someone you care about, knows someone and loves someone like Aristides. Too often, our society seems to think that former inmates and incarcerated people don't have stories worth telling. Or we think that prison, isn't enough of a punishment for various misdeeds. Instead, we feel the need to strip them of all dignity, and security. We either ignore or actively advocate for policies and conditions that are cruel, unjust and inhumane. We do things, that frankly, we would call out if another nation was doing the same.

We deliberately and callously strip inmates of both their identities and their families through policies that dehumanize them and punish their families for loving them. This is the biggest mistake we could ever make. Aristides and others like him can only return as functional members of society with the love and support of people that care about them. When we deny conjugal visitations or meaningful interaction between incarcerated individuals and their loved ones, we break up families. An inmate without a family, is more likely to re-offend and more likely to return to prison. A child with an incarcerated parent is more likely to grow up in poverty, and more likely be incarcerated themselves as an adult. According to the United

States Department of Justice, 1 child in 50 has a parent in prison, which is 5 million children.

Unfortunately, the decisions that we make on how we choose to punish people in our society are politically drive, not based on decades of research. These decisions also reflect on who we are as a society and what we will tolerate. It won't get any better until we demand that it does.

# Marnie Gellhorn

# Glossary

*Aseodores* – inmates who clean the prison

*Mechanics* – inmates that are responsible for fixing any mechanical prison equipment, vehicles

*Pasilleros* – the inmates who control the patio.

*Patio* – term for prison housing unit, used similar to tier in American multi-level facilities

*Pinche* – food prisoners buy outside of prison issued meals

*Socio* – prison friend, short for associo, or associate

*Rancheros* – inmates who worked as prison cooks. This is one of the better jobs

*Wimpi* – slang term for food from the prison kitchen

# Chapter 1: Guilty in all ways but one

My name is Aristides Jesus Gonzalez Riohacha, and my prison number was #0903277, and this is my story.

I know that the many of the people in my position protest their innocence. Enough so that it's become almost standard fare. I am certainly guilty of something; of that I do not protest. However, I am less guilty of the crime from which I was charged than I am of being ignorant.

I was born and raised in the fantastic, sprawling yet crumbling megalith that is Colombia's capital city, Bogota. Within this massive ever enlarging city, there are a myriad of smaller cities, townships and neighborhoods. You can wander thru the sprawling rat warren of the poorest neighborhoods, where cement-block steady houses tower, juxtaposed with lean-tos and other make-do dwellings of recycled, ransacked and salvaged materials of hard plastic sheeting, brick, metal barrels and packed dirt, all covered with tarp. From here, you can see the snaking cables that provide electricity and often even internet to even the humblest of abodes. Within these networks, in small corner bodegas the aroma of freshly made tamales, and arepas along with the ever-present dark coffee is a whisper on the wind. This along with the frequent rains help to wash away the other, less pleasant scents of poverty; of hastily dumped trash, rotting and ravaged by stray animals who, thusly fed and satisfied, relieve themselves in the narrow, and cracked streets of South Bogota, of Cazuca, La Colmena or Caracoli. These streets thrum with life, as young men sit on the corners, smoking cigarettes and drinking hot, steamy, tiny cups of tinto, with their motorcycles and bicycles standby. They wait for the call to action, on their phones thru the various apps, ready to go, with their delivery boxes strapped to their backs. Various venders walk by with the carts, with the call of "Aguacate! Aguacate!" calling shoppers to them. Others, wait with their modernized rickshaws and gypsy cabs to take busy and harried workers farther to the north, to their employers' middle class homes and establishments. These neighborhoods snake up into the hills on the edges of the mountains that rim the city.

Here in Usaquen, the buildings are taller, and the signs are cleaner. High rises, and fancy medical clinics, and shopping malls interspersed with proud brick apartment buildings and the older, but still elegant conjuntos of the middle-class. Through it all runs the Transmileno, Bogota's famed bus system. At times crowded to the point of bursting, it remains the mainstay of transportation for most of the city. The city streets remain chronically congested as a plethora of cars, trucks, other buses, bicycles, motorcycles and newer forms of transportation clog all of the main arteries, most of the time, despite aggressive measures meant to curb the long lines of traffic that make traffic in Bogota one of the worst in the world.

Above the fray, literally, in elegant apartment buildings and grandiose homes perched above the Septima, one of main streets of the city, lies the homes of the wealthy. While these homes climb the hills, they avoid the precarious nature of the casas de invasion, or the rudely built and jerry-rigged dwellings of the poor. The inhabitants of these homes know an entirely different Bogota than the rest of us. The politicians, artists, singers and (sometimes) nefarious businessmen that live here know little of the day to day worries of the rest of the city. Even, if they once knew, they have spent considerable time and effort to forget, from behind the high walls, electrified fences and patrolled residences. Armed guards sit in bulletproof gatehouses to protect these residences from these awkward reminders.

For most of my life, I fell somewhere in the lower middle of the widening morass of Bogota society. I grew up in the working-class area of Barrio Bachue, living with my mother and my sister in a tidy and cozy apartment within a network of tiny streets inaccessible by car. My mother, having divorced my father when I was an adolescent, supported my sister and I as a seamstress and was well-known in the community for her curtains, upholstery and other home furnishing work.

As a young man, I had engaged myself in a steady if varied number of increasingly skilled trades. I was never without work, for long. Here in Colombia, work isn't always guaranteed, and upward social mobility isn't determined by anything other than the availability of opportunity. For many Colombians in barrios like mine, hard work has no role in the success or failure of an individual or their family. The hard work and the struggle is a given.

I'd also engaged in a number of romantic relationships, some of them more turbulent than others. With an easy-going nature, a portion of charm and good looks, I was never without female company for long. I'd emerged from one such turbulent relationship with my baby daughter, Sara and was determined to avoid the often-stereotyped drama of high maintenance women. Sara's mother, Diana, still stalked and harassed me at ever available turn, in a warped bid to get me to return to her. But just as her continual screaming, ranting and raving had made it impossible for me to stay with her, it made it equally unattractive to return. Diana Consuelo Pena Farjardo had been beautiful when I'd first met her, thin, light complexed with blonde hair and big flashing eyes. When I first met her, she had been friendly, and polite with a three-year-old daughter, Dana, in tow. But once we were together, too often those dark eyes flashed with jealousy and a violent fury. Her almost constant rage twisted her features and contorted her into something I didn't recognize. I did my best to maintain ties with my darling daughter even as Diana manipulated and schemed to use the baby to keep me close.

I was determined not to make the same mistake in my next serious relationship. I believed I had succeeded when I met the elegant, and well-educated Chilean beauty, Andrea Isabel Olivos Vedugo. Unlike Diana, who was from my own neighborhood, Andrea was exotic, and she was different from any other women I'd ever known. I was working at the Hotel Dann, as a private chauffeur when I met her. She had an eye-catching figure that attracted the attention of several of the men at the hotel. I was flattered by her attention. I didn't know it then, but she was to become my worst nightmare.

She was here in Bogota for a conference, working for the Chilean government. She had trained as a librarian and was an excellent conversationalist on a variety of topics. At the time, I thought she was graceful, smart, funny and very, very charming. She had a sexy laugh that brought fire to her eyes. At the same time, she seemed to lack that irrational jealous streak that Diana possessed. Very quickly, I became enamored of Andrea. When she returned to Chile, we remained in constant contact. We would travel back and forth to see each other, and I fell deeply in love. This only served to enrage Diana, who made it her personal mission to ensure that I was never happy again. Diana was full of spite and misplaced vengeance. "If I can't have him," was more than her philosophy, it seemed to be her reason for being. She had already sabotaged several of my budding relationships with stalking and threats, but now she devoted herself to making Andrea's life a misery with a vigor I'd never seen before. She'd even gone as far as contacting Andrea's employer in Santiago, Chile with the false claims that Andrea had interfered with our (nonexistent) marriage and was "breaking up a family." Andrea's boss didn't care about the truth of the matter, he didn't want to deal with any scandals or problems, and so she lost her job shortly after.

This changed everything between us because now I felt responsible for her situation. I remember feeling such a strong feeling of love and affection for her when she would proudly present me to her friends and colleagues at numerous social events. I was proud of her looking past my humble roots and loving the man inside. When she lost her job, because of Diana's actions, I felt horrible. I was enraged at Diana and fought with her as I never had before. I felt helpless and impotent. I had always been a calm, methodical and rational person, and I didn't know how to deal with Diana's actions. I yelled at her, but otherwise kept my emotions inside, where they ate at my stomach lining.

Andrea soon returned to Bogota, to be with me and found a position working in a local university. I thought this meant that we could conquer any obstacle and we decided to marry. Of course, I didn't know any of this until much later. So, we married, and for a time, I thought we were happy.

But within six months, Andrea became very controlling, yet secretive. She was possessive and jealous, calling me at work at all hours, demanding that I return home for invented emergencies. When I arrived, out of breath and harried, she'd brush off my questions and pretend that she'd never called. Eventually, her frequent emergencies and constant phone calls got me fired, which is what she wanted. She wanted me to be with her all day, every day on a very short leash.

It seemed that all of the things I loved about Andrea were an illusion, and that she was more like Diana that I could have ever imaged. Her jealousy and possessiveness made Diana look like an amateur. When we were in the car, she would accuse me of looking at other women at the traffic lights. She would go through my cellphone messages in the early morning while I was sleeping. She frequently accused me of cheating on her whenever I wasn't with her. She alienated all of my friends and became more and more obsessive. She tried to keep me from my child because she thought that I was sleeping with Diana.

At the same time, phones calls and messages to Andrea would go unanswered for hours. My mother stopped by our new apartment in Teusaquillo several times while I was working, only to find the apartment dark and vacant. Back then, I brushed off my mother's concerns. She voiced her suspicions to me a couple of times, but I told her to leave us alone.

She and Andrea had never gotten along well. My mother felt that Andrea was very condescending towards her. Andrea had rebuffed all of my mother's attempts to incorporate her into the family. To Andrea's credit, she always gave me the impression that she wanted a close relationship with my family but that it somehow eluded her. I thought that maybe she was uncomfortable with the close intimacy of my family. My mother was one of ten children, so her apartment was always full of uncles, aunts, and a plentitude of rowdy children. Andrea came from a small somewhat distant family, and her own daughter lived with her parents. Eventually, this led to me becoming more distant with my own family. We no longer attended my family's weekend get-togethers and picnics. It was just easier that way, to avoid problems. But you can only avoid confrontation for so long, and this was my greatest crime. I thought if I ignored all the signs that something strange was going on, that somehow it would all work out okay.

It came to a head in 2015 when I left my phone on the kitchen counter. I received a couple of texts from Diana regarding my visitation with Sarita. Andrea, of course was snooping in my phone and went ballistic. She was screaming and crying, and carrying on. I could no longer ignore the fact that our relationship had real problems. Frankly, I was tired of being a prisoner to my wife. Of course, I didn't know how true that would turn out to be. But I was tired of all the drama, the screaming, the accusations. I told her I was leaving, I couldn't do this anymore.

Her long, claw-like manicured nails were like sharp knives as she raked them across my face. I step back, completed shocked by her violent attack. She'd screamed at me before, multiple times, but she'd never physically attacked me before. I turned to leave, disgusted by the violence. She began slapping and hitting me as she screamed, "stop hurting me" at the top of her lungs. I held her at arm's length as I tried to sidestep her assault.

"Stop!" I said, completely dismayed to see my wife acting like this. I moved to leave the apartment, as she tried to block me. I just had a moment to react as she lunged at me. I quickly pushed her away and fled the apartment. I went to a nearby bodega to calm down.

I was shaking as I called the police for help. I wanted them to accompany me back to the apartment to get some of things. They came with me a few days later. But for now, I didn't intent to spend another night with the woman who had been deceiving me since the day we met. When the police arrived the next day, I felt a little humiliated as they accompanied me back to the apartment, but I wasn't taking any chances. But when we arrived, the apartment was dark, and there was no sign of Andrea. Most of her things were there, but she had taken all of our legal documents, including our marriage certificate. She also took a bag of our sex toys. She had a wide range of kinky activities she enjoyed, so we had a fairly extensive collection.

I quickly packed a bag and left. I was embarrassed, but grateful when my mother answered the door and embraced me without asking questions. The next day, I returned with family, and packed all of my things and left. I didn't see Andrea then, for which I was grateful. The day after that, Andrea started calling and sending messages, but I ignored her. I 'd had enough.

I did the only thing I knew how to, to cope, I went to work. I worked extra shifts and did my best to forget about it and move on. Later, I received messages from a local social worker, that Andrea had consulted, saying she wanted to reconcile with me. Andrea began sending people to my mother's house to try and get me to see her. Finally, I agreed to meet with Andrea and the social worker, after repeated messages but despite several scheduled meetings, Andrea never showed up.

What none of us realized, is that this was all part of her plan. She was angry, crazy angry and she was going to make me pay. I'd like to think that at some point in the process, she at least felt bad about what she was about to do, but there's absolutely no evidence of that. Instead, she went to a very close friend who worked in the forensic medicine division, which is Colombia's legal medicine department. She had her friend certify that I had been abusive and beat her. She had been telling this friend all kinds of lies during our marriage, saying I was cheating, that I was hitting her, and hurting her. I didn't know any of this at the time, and I carried on with my life. We had agreed to get divorced, and she was supposed to bring the papers for me to sign, but she never did. I didn't have the time or money to play these games with her, so I never sought a divorce on my own.

Two years later, I had finally met someone who loved me for me. Her name was Yajaira Sanchez Robaya, and she loved me wholeheartedly. She healed me and she restored my faith. She had no ulterior motives, she just wanted to share her life with me. She was beautiful, inside and out. She was a petite but voluptuous women who had a smile that could brighten a room, and I felt pure joy when I was in her arms. She had streaky blonde hair and lovely expressive green eyes. I met her at my brother-in-law's birthday party. She was a friend of his cousin, and she emoted caring and compassion like a perfume. I needed that, desperately.

We decided to make a fresh start, so we moved to Pereira. She had an uncle there, and he helped us find jobs and an apartment when we moved there. Everything was going well in Pereira, until it wasn't.

I was working in the regional office of Avis rental cars, and life was looking up. I had stable employment and was in the process of being promoted. Yajaira was at my side, and she was wise, kind and loving. Diana was back to her usual tactics, but Yajaira just ignored her. She worked for an airline, and she too, was climbing the corporate ladder. She had no interest in the games Diana liked to play, and her boss laughed at Diana's transparent attempts to manipulate him.

One day, in 2018, I was at work, when I suddenly began to have terrible stomach pain. I was nauseated and felt faint. I started sweating profusely, and my colleagues called an ambulance. I was admitted into the hospital, with Yajaira at my side. In just a few hours, I had become incredibly sick. I drifted in and out of consciousness. Between the illness and the medicines that the nurses were giving me for my abdominal pain, I was sleepy and sedated much of the time.

Yajaira left my bedside only to go to the airport to pick up my mom. In that brief period, I woke up in the darkened room, alone. My cellphone, on my bedside table was tinging with incoming messages. As I picked up my phone, *her* name flashed with the incoming messages.

"Mi amor, perdoname," she wrote. "But I need to know you are okay. Please just let me know you are okay, and I won't contact you again." That was how Monica came back into my life. I don't know how she knew I was sick – she later swore she had no idea, "just a feeling" but as I sat afraid, alone in my hospital room, I answered her. She called me immediately and began crying, which was the last thing I'd expected from this strong willed and determined woman.

Her first question was to ask if there was anyone to take care of me, "Please tell me you aren't all alone," she said. I think I wanted to hurt her, the way she had hurt me when she'd left me. So, I readily told her about Yajaira, my loving angel.

"Thank God," she said, with relief evident in her voice. In that moment, I forgave her, for everything. She hung up after getting assurances that Yajaira and my mom were on the way to the hospital, and a promise to update her on my condition. She was never gone from my life after that. She didn't interfere with Yajaira and I, she stayed quietly in the background. She made no promises, and neither did I. I was slowly recovering, with my beloved Yajaira at my side. But later, when my world collapsed, it was Monica Marie Dale who propped me up and waited for me.

As I recovered from the acute hepatitis that had almost killed me, I received a legal summons to appear in court. After all this time, Andrea had decided to extract her pound of flesh. The summons had taken a few weeks to reach me in Pereira, after arriving at my mother's house. By the time, I had received it, the court date had passed. I returned to Bogota, and contacted a lawyer, but after receiving a hefty consultation fee, he advised me to return to Pereira while he contacted the court. With the matter in hand, or so I thought, I went back to Yajaira and my life in Pereria, with no hint of what was about to happen. While my lawyer dawdled and played around, I unwittingly missed another court appearance.

Several months later, Yajaira and I had returned to Bogota. Her beloved uncle in Pereira had died of stomach cancer, which is endemic in Colombia. Her aging parents were ill with a variety of ailments, and she needed to be closer to them. I was at El Dorado Airport, picking up clients when the police first arrested me. That was my first indication that something more serious than divorce proceedings was going on. I was held in a communal cell in the anti-narcotics unit near the airport for over a week before being transferred to an administrative unit at the prison. I had been tried and sentenced in absentia to eight years incarceration, and now I was being transported to the most infamous prison in Colombia to serve my time. It turned out that my so-called lawyer, Armando Vaquero had intentionally advised me to ignore the summons while he privately met with the court. I never had the opportunity to face my accuser or defend myself from false testimony. I could have easily defended myself from most of the accusations, I even had a police report to support my side of the story. But it probably wouldn't have mattered. Andrea had gone to a friend of her lover's, a federal prosecutor with a wild tale of marital abuse, and the prosecutor had seized on the opportunity to make an example of me. Colombia's Department of Justice and State attorney had declared war on domestic violence, and I was to be it's first victim. Another friend of Andrea's powerful new partner worked as a state forensic physician, and it was she that made the report than damned me. But even as it was, the evidence was nonexistence. The only thing the forensic physician had seized on was a 1 mm freckle on Andrea's arm. For this, she proclaimed was evidence of abuse, resulting in five days of 'incapcidad', when Andrea was supposedly too ill to work, function or care for herself. There were no hospital records to submit, obviously, as no hospital would admit a perfectly healthy and uninjured woman for a one-millimeter freckle on his right bicep.

But it didn't matter, with my lawyer in cahoots, I had lost any opportunity to appeal. My family had also lost a large amount of money, which they had used to pay to the lawyer to retain him.

# Chapter 2: La Picota

My first days in La Picota were the worst. I was still in a state of disbelief which changed to deep depression as the realization of the truth of my situation set in. Time is relative in prison, and while books, and movies always portray time as endless in prison, it didn't seem that way to me. Instead, I found there was no time to mourn, no time to grieve. Instead, I was thrust away from everything I'd ever known, and forced to maintain constant vigilance to survive. I felt afraid, of what would happen to me in prison, of what would happen to my family while I was away, and afraid for my future. I couldn't even imagine what my future would be like. I was also deeply angry at Andrea for her cruel lies, my horrible lawyer for his deception and at myself, for allowing this to happen. This anger was fed by my frustration at my inability to do anything to help the situation. It seemed like everything I did just made it worse. All of this fed into an overwhelming and enormous sense of hopelessness.

After I was apprehended at the airport, I was transported to La Picota. The man next to me on the van was named Alex Duran. Alex was a 28-year-old man who had been extradited from Panama back to Colombia.

We started talking about our lack of experience and prison smarts and decided we would stick together. We made a pact to look out for each other on the long ride over. We were herded into a huge room with about 300 other detainees when we arrived. A group of openly homosexual men pranced in, with several sets of clippers. They were in the in-house barbers. We were lined up and shaved. Men with beards and mustaches had those shaved too. As they prepared us to have our official prison photo taken, I heard several inmates laughing and joking. They kept telling me that "your brother is over here." With that ignoble introduction, I came face to face with another man, who did look remarkably like me. His name was Blake, and we quickly decided that we should use our fraternal relationship in our favor. Blake quickly became the third partner in our alliance. We each agreed to take turns sleeping and watching guard, over each other and our limited possessions, including our newly issued blankets.

After spending the whole day in that crowded space, we were marched across prison grounds. It was dark and cold, and it seemed like we marched forever, until we reached a large hanger like building. Inside the building were several smaller cells. As we were crowded into the cells, Alex, Blake and I made sure that we ended up in the same cell. Just as we had settled into the cell, the guards turned out the lights. Then came the terrifying sound of dozens if not hundreds of rats scurrying and racing across the beams over our heads. They weren't aggressive. They didn't try to approach or attack anyone, but the clicking of their nails along ceiling along with the scrapes and scratching were deeply unsettling. We kept to our plan to take turns on watch, but it was hard to settle down to sleep when it was my turn. It was cold, uncomfortable, and frightening to be cramped in the cell with a group of strangers.

The next day, we had our medical exams before we were assigned to our patios. We were then led, single file into structure one, the older area of the prison that housed the medium security unit. As we were led in, the catcalls from the other inmates within the patios started. They started yelling that they were going to "fuck us," and "fresh meat.[1]" It was even worse, as we marched into the hallway that led to the housing units. It was dark and poorly lit, and the inmates were just a few feet away as they yelled at us. As we turned the corner into one darkened area, I felt pure terror as we passed an area that used back in the 1980's and the 1990's to kidnap, murder and dismember prisoners[2]. I could feel all of the evil negative energy emanating from there and I wanted to get as far away from that area as possible. Finally, we reached our housing unit.

In a strange set of circumstances, the person who helped me the most to stay safe was Diana. I don't know if it was a perverse sense of guilt or merely a desire to maintain a father for her child, but the erratic and irrational Diana was the person who stepped forward to ease my path in La Picota. She reached out to an old friend, whose father was a lawyer to help arrange for my placement in a better part of the prison. He arranged with some of the guards to have me transferred to that area.

Alex had been assigned to Patio Seven, but Blake and I were fortunate enough to be assigned to the same patio, Patio Six. I was now officially an inmate of La Picota.

*Part of La Picota prison structure. Photo courtesy of INPEC*

# Chapter 3: Patio Six

La Picota is one of the most infamous prisons in Colombia. It is located on the southern edge of Bogota, where the weather tends to be colder and wetter. This is accentuated in the ancient part of the prison where I was housed. La Picota is famous for all of the wrong reasons, much like the Attica Correctional Facility in upstate New York. Violent prison riots often spurred by inhumane conditions, corrupt guards and scandalous escapes mar the reputation of this place. The maximum-security ward is filled with drug traffickers, their paid assassins (sicarios), and other dangerous criminals. There is a VIP wing called R- Sur that houses the many Colombian politicians including mayors, governors, senators and cabinet ministers, even presidents that drift in and out on various charges of corruption[3]. It's not as comfortable or as cozy as Pablo Escobar's private prison, the infamous La Cathedral, outside Medellin, but these VIPS have been certainly known to get more than "three hots and a cot" while staying here. Their incarceration has also not served as much of a barrier to their re-entry into the political arena in many cases, either. Our current president, Gustavo Petro, is a pretty good example of that[4]. Of course, he was in Modelo Prison in Bogota, which is a terrifying facility that houses terrorists, paramilitaries and guerillas; because he was of course, a member of a violent paramilitary group[5].

Nowadays, they like to whitewash his participation, and play up the fact that he joined as a teenager, and used a name based on one of the characters of Gabriel Garcia Marquez, one of Colombia's most famous romantic novelists. But the truth of it was, he was part of M-19, which was a violent left-wing group responsible for multiple murders and hostage taking. They were also involved in the thefts of large numbers of weapons which they used to arm their members. Gustavo Petro was convicted and sentenced for his role in weapons thefts. At the very peak of his involvement, (and just after his incarceration), M-19 perpetrated its biggest attack against the people of our country, during the siege at the Palace of Justice in late 1985. During the siege, the terrorist organization took over 300 people hostage including the entire supreme court, and multiple other judges, and lawyers. The ensuing events which included a raid by the army, lead to the deaths of over 100 people, and over half of the Supreme Court justices. Coincidentally, or maybe less so, the attack commenced just as the supreme court was getting ready to decide on the constitutionality of the US- Colombia extradition treaty which was being actively used and threatened against members of the Medellin (and other Colombian) drug cartels. Many people that M-19 was paid by the cartels to destroy the court to prevent that decision from taking place.

Gustavo Petro wasn't at the Palace of Justice that day since he was serving part of his short 16-month sentence. I find that ironic, but also emblematic of this country. A domestic terrorist actively involved in obtaining illegal weapons serves 16 months. I married the wrong woman and end up with an eight-year sentence. He's now the President of Colombia, and I am struggling to find steady work due to my history as former inmate. In Spanish, inmates are called 'Condemnados,' and I find this to be unerringly accurate. For the rest of us, non-VIPs, serving time in prison condemns us for life.

The original section of La Picota was build in 1936, and this is the area where I was housed. If you are picturing a big crumbling, cold concrete building with thick iron bars on the doors and windows, like Alcatraz, then you have it about right. There are newer sections like the maximum-security area, and they are currently expanding the prison even further, but I lived in the old, almost historic area. The building is divided into seven areas, or patios. The direct translation of "patio" into English, is Yard, but it really is a cement-covered open-air space that defines each of the housing units, so "Patio" still seems the most appropriate.

Patio Six is the farthest area in the old structure from the entrance, as you follow a winding hallway past the other areas.

If this were a movie, the men of Patio Six would be a group of loveable misfits or something of the sort. We weren't worst of the lot, as I've already mentioned those inmates were housed in the maximum-security structure adjacent to ours, but we weren't a bunch of misunderstood teddy bears either. Patio Six is the patio (or housing unit) that housed most of the non-Colombian prisoners. When I arrived, there were about two hundred inmates on the patio, but after the release of large numbers of prisoners during covid[6], and other accelerated releases due to overcrowding, there were only about one hundred of us when I was released on parole. Patio Six housed a motley assortment of foreigners as well as the occasional Colombian, like myself, who managed to bribe or solicit their way onto this patio.

I later found out that the Mexican actor, Diego Catano Elizondo was in La Picota at the same time I was, on similar charges, but despite being a foreigner, he never ended up on Patio Six. He's famous for being in the Netflix series, "Narcos" playing a Colombian character, La Quica (based on Dandeny Muñoz Mosquera) of the Medellin cartel. He ended up requesting an expedited extradition back to Mexico, and left before any of us really knew he was here.

# The Pasilleros

nce we entered Patio Six, we had to pass through the main corridor. This corridor was controlled by two 'Pasilleros', Pepsi and Luis. Pepsi is a rolo, or a Bogota native. He is 37 years old, a short, fat white man. Luis is a tall 34-year-old Venezuelan who was convicted of drug trafficking. He works out on the patio most days, so he's well-build and heavily muscled. Both men have multiple tattoos on their chests and biceps. They make a menacing duo. As Pasajeros, they are some of the most powerful people in the unit. Pasajeros are usually people with the most seniority on the unit, and the longest sentences.

They inform us that the toll to enter the passageway is 35,000 pesos per person[7]. This doesn't include monthly "cleaning fees" of 5,000 pesos or a television use fee of 3,000 pesos. I quickly contacted my mother to have her transfer the funds electronically. Technically, you don't have to pay to be on Patio Six. No one will hurt you or kill you if you don't. But, if you don't pay the toll, the Pasilleros won't allow you to enter the main corridor. People who don't pay are forced to stay in another area of the Patio until they either pay, or they end up being sent to other patios. On the other patios, the tax system is more readily enforced. People who don't pay the entry tax are beaten until they pay.

Once Blake and I have paid to pass into the corridor, we still don't have a place the sleep. The patio is very overcrowded, so all of the cells are fully occupied. People find anywhere they can to sleep. Blake and I are fortunate to find a space in the main corridor, other people are sleeping by the toilets that often overflow with filth. It's horribly cold, especially in the early morning on the floor and it's difficult to rest.

My dad holds a raffle in the city of Sopo, where he lives. He offers a new radio as a prize. He sends me the money so I can buy a cell when one of the other prisoners is released. Once I have a cell, I invite Blake to use the other bunk in the room. Blake is my cellmate until he's released several months later. After that, I have a series of cellmates.

The prison is filthy despite all of our efforts to clean. It's hard to keep anything clean when the fungus and mold abound in the moist conditions. Fecal contamination, both human and animal of both the food and the water has led to further outbreaks of diarrheal disease. Inadequate toilet facilities led to increasingly unhygienic conditions. An acute lack of fresh water during several episodes at La Picota means that even basic sanitary measures like handwashing are unavailable. We resort to using cups, buckets and any other containers we can find to collect rainwater to drink.

There is a menagerie of animals in La Picota, which only adds to the disorder. Massive rats that are the same size as rabbits and small cats are frequently seen, scavenging thru the prison. The severe rat infestations throughout the prison lead to fleas, illnesses and other skin infections. Rat infestations have led to several outbreaks of Leptospira and other diseases in the prison. The general lack of sanitation also causes to outbreaks of dysentery, and a virulent bacterial infection that results in amputations of infected limbs in several inmates[8].

I am constantly sick and develop a severe skin rash on my extremities. Then several of my teeth begin to rot. I haven't been able to see a dentist since I was arrested. The doctors and nurses that are assigned to La Picota don't come. We have no access to medical care, except for a limited amount of medicines and creams that the prison guards will allow our families to send in care packages. Monica sends vitamins and creams for my rashes.

Several dogs also live at the prison, including Aurelio, a 12- or 13-year-old mutt that is much appreciated for his prolific rat-killing ability. He's an expert at rat extermination and is able to ferret out rat enclaves. Aurelio doesn't eat the rats but frequently goes on killing sprees, ranging thru the patios looking for rats, tearing them apart and then tossing them aside. Aurelio and his fellow dogs are an important part of La Picota. The inmates take good care of the dogs. When a pregnant dog comes to Patio 6 to give birth, the inmates are happy to look after the eight tiny puppies. Some of the puppies were adopted by the guards. The remainder were adopted by families of the inmates.

One of the bootshiners on our patio, "Migajas," who was serving a 30-year sentence for extortion gave one of the puppies to his wife and son. They took the puppy home and would send pictures of the growing dog. Migajas did the same after he was initially released, before dying of a cocaine overdose.

# Popeye

The Pasilleros aren't the only people that I met on Patio Six. There's "Popeye," a fifty-year-old man who is serving a 35-year sentence for a series of crimes including kidnapping, robbery and murder. He's a career criminal, who has been working with different criminal gangs since he was a teenager. He's not in a "regular" or part of one of the many Colombian gangs that run the streets. He's a freelance agent, who works for anyone that will pay him.

He's been in and out of several other prisons since the age of 20. He's tall, over 6'2" fair skinned, with blue eyes. He's bald, with missing teeth and very muscular. He has numerous tattoos of skulls, serpents and other dark symbols. He currently works as a farmer in the prison farm along with five other people from Patio Six. It's a great prison job because it gives Popeye access to fresh food that he can skim off to sell or trade. Despite his alarming history, I spend a lot of time listening to Popeye and his numerous stories about his previous adventures and experiences in other prisons. I doesn't talk much to Popeye, but I do like to listen. It helps pass the time and keeps my mind from the dark, depressing thoughts. I can't keep them out completely, but sometimes if I keep busy enough, I can forget for an hour or two.

# Chi- Chi

ngel "Chi – Chi" Calisto is a 48-year-old from Costa Rica. He has big eyes and a big mouth. He kind of looks like one of the characters from that animated movie, "Ice Age," with his big cauliflower ears, tiny, flared nose. He's what we call "Mas feo que horrible.[9]"

He was transporting marijuana on a boat from Costa Rica to Jamaica. He has the misfortune to travel through Colombian waters on his route, where he was detained by the Colombian coast guard. But if it hadn't happened on that occasion, it would have happened eventually. He was sentenced to nine years and was initially imprisoned on the Colombian island of San Aristides before being transferred to La Picota.

Chi-Chi is an asshole. He's a fisherman by trade but a thief by nature. He likes to steal, and often steals to feed his crack addiction. When he's not stealing, he can manage to hold down a normal job for long periods of time. As a fisherman, he knows that there is an area of jet stream turbulence off the Costa Rican coast. This is where many of the drug shipments that have to be jettisoned mid-transport end up, due to the prevailing currents. One day, he and several friends found a suitcase full of cocaine. He was able to sell the suitcase for the equivalent of 500 million pesos[10]. To celebrate his score, Chi-Chi embarked on an 8-day crack binge with several prostitutes, spending over thirty thousand dollars.

But he didn't blow thru all the money, right away. He was smart enough to use most of the money to buy himself a house and used the money to pay for it in full. He stopped working for the next few months and after limiting himself to marijuana only, was suddenly seized with an irresistible urge to smoke crack. Once he started smoking crack again, there was no stopping Chi-Chi. He smoked crack day and night, running up a huge crack debt with the local dealers until one day, the dealers forced him out of his house, and re-possessed it as payment. But Chi-Chi isn't just a thief with a taste for crack. He's a vicious and vindictive man with a long history of criminal behavior. He was in prison on three separate occasions while in Costa Rica for armed robbery. His favorite modis operandi is to hijack trucks by running up and putting a gun to the driver's head. He also brags that he killed an enemy back in Costa Rica, a man that snitched on him in the past. He killed him in a fight but managed to evade criminal charges. He likes to say that he was never told not to do things as a kid, and that this lack of discipline was instrumental to his career stealing, robbing and attacking people, even as a young juvenile. Bad as it all is, the real reason, I think he's a total asshole is because he used to go into the Costa Rican National Turtle Reserve and wait for the turtles to lay their eggs. Then he would steal and sell both the turtles and their eggs. This really bothers me. The stuff about drugs and robberies, well, that's most of the people here, but selling endangered animals to be killed and eaten is just terrible.

While he was in La Picota, Chi-Chi got into the mattress/tent-making and motel business. He would sew mattresses and tents as part of the prison industry and then sell some of the mattresses to guards and other inmates. It was good money, particularly when he combined it with his "motel" business.

La Picota and most of the other prisons in Colombia allow conjugal visits between inmates and their significant others[11]. These visits are generally scheduled for every other Sunday (prior to the pandemic). On those Sundays, Chi-Chi would set up tents with mattresses, that provide privacy for many of the couples. These were called motels. These motels rented for 15 thousand pesos for the duration of the visit. But Chi-Chi began selling drugs in the prison, and quickly reignited his crack addiction. Once he started smoking crack again, he was no longer interested in running the mattress business. I had already started learning how to sew mattresses and tents. I was able to use some of the money I had saved before I went to prison to buy his mattress and motel business. It was a good way for me to make money and I didn't have to muscle in on anyone. I used a lot of the money I made after taking over Chi-Chi's business to buy fresh food, and meat to eat. That's a real priority here because a lot of the prison food that they serve to you is rotten and inedible[12].

I was later able to use the money I made from the sale of ten mattresses and ten tents to bribe a guard to help me submit my paperwork to the judge for my early release into the house arrest program. If I hadn't given the guard money, my paperwork would have languished somewhere. Instead, I am here at my mother's house, telling you my story.

# El Diablo

His name is Jean Pastor Aguillar Tapias but we call him the devil because of what he did. He's the oldest inmate in La Picota, which is why he's in Patio Six. El Diablo is 83 when I met him and is known to be extremely grumpy when he's out of cigarettes. He works as the garbage man for the patio. He's from a small town near La Vega, Cundinamarca. He was the well tolerated town alcoholic, spending his days drinking Chicha and Guarapo all day long. The town is small enough that people overlook his chronic drunkenness, especially as he seems to be good natured and full of entertaining stories. That is until he wakes up after a bender one morning the small bodega where he works with his hand still holding the knife that is sticking out of his dead son-in-law. He's been at La Picota for nine years, with twenty-two more to go. He was initially sentenced to thirty-six years, but his sentence was reduced due to his advanced age. His story just seems sad to me. Other than being habitually drunk, he'd never committed a crime prior to this.

# Jorge Armando Arca Barrigo

Jorge was sentenced to 261 months in La Picota for kidnapping but managed to get out before I did. Despite his crime, Jorge was a good guy and a good friend to me. He certainly didn't look like a kidnapper or a convicted criminal. He looked like an accountant. He was thin, medium height, with glasses. He often served as my own personal jailhouse lawyer, advisor and confidante. He helped me hand write the solicitations to the court, including the petition for my early release based on my good time credits. Without his help, I'd still be there. He's the only person from the prison that I stay in contact with.

Bogotá 31 Enero de 2022.
Establecimiento Carcelario y Penitenciario de Bogotá.

Señores:
C.E.T.
Consejo de Evaluación y Tratamiento.

Referencia: Derecho de Petición
(Artículo 23 c.u)

Asunto: Solicitud Clasificación Fase Mínima Seguridad

Respetables señores: [ilegible] TD # 0327 , patio # 6
Estructura 1, me dirijo muy formalmente a su dependencia con
el [ilegible] se [ilegible] por [ilegible] se me corrrecta la Clasificación
Notificación del Acta de Mínima Seguridad, como lo establece
el artículo 144 ley 65/93 y la resolución 7302 de 2005.
Soy un interno condenado a la pena de 72 meses, de los cuales he
descontado 30 meses físicos y una redención requisito de
4 meses, 9 días, tiempo que cumple el requisito [ilegible] para ser
clasificado en la fase mencionada.
• No poseo informes disciplinarios.
• He llevado a cabo la asistencia a los cursos psicosociales progra-
mados en la fase de Mediana Seguridad.
Por lo tanto ruego se lleve a cabo la entrevista est. pilado ppm
del fin, y se me establezca para continuar el sistema de seguimiento
progresivo que avala el tratamiento penitenciario adecuado.

Respetuosamente:

patio #6 Estructura 1
TD # 0327
NUI # [ilegible]

Example of handwritten petition

# Ralph "the Gringo"

If there is anyone on the patio that I really don't like, it's Ralph. I don't remember his last name, but I sure wish I did. I think that everyone who reads this book should be on the lookout to keep their families safe from Ralph. He's the only person from the United States on the patio when I get there. He's from Maryland, and he taught English classes when he was at La Picota. He is an older, grey-haired, mild-mannered looking, potbellied man but he's a life-long child molester. He served a long sentence in Colombia for child molestation and child pornography and was released on probation. He then attempted to flee Colombia but the plane developed problems mid-flight and had to return to Bogota. When the flight landed, he was apprehended for violating his probation. He was sentenced to La Picota to serve the rest of his time. He's a nice enough fellow in a regular sort of way, which is what I find the most disturbing, and what makes me dislike him. If I didn't know him any better, I'd think he was just another of the many gringo retirees that settle in places like Rionegro or Medellin, where their pensions go farther than it would in Boca Raton. The kind of guy that wears khaki cargo shorts, a Senor Frog t-shirt from a previous Mexican vacation, along with black socks and sandals everywhere. He's the kind of guy that you see so often, you no longer even see him.

When I was a driver and private tour guide, I drove people like him around all the time, to tourist sites like La Candelaria, Monserrate, or the Salt Cathedral in Zipaquira.

It also makes me frustrated that he gets out sooner than I do. He's a serial molester, and the sooner he gets back out there, the sooner he can abuse another child. When I think about him abusing children younger than my little daughter, it makes me feel physically ill.

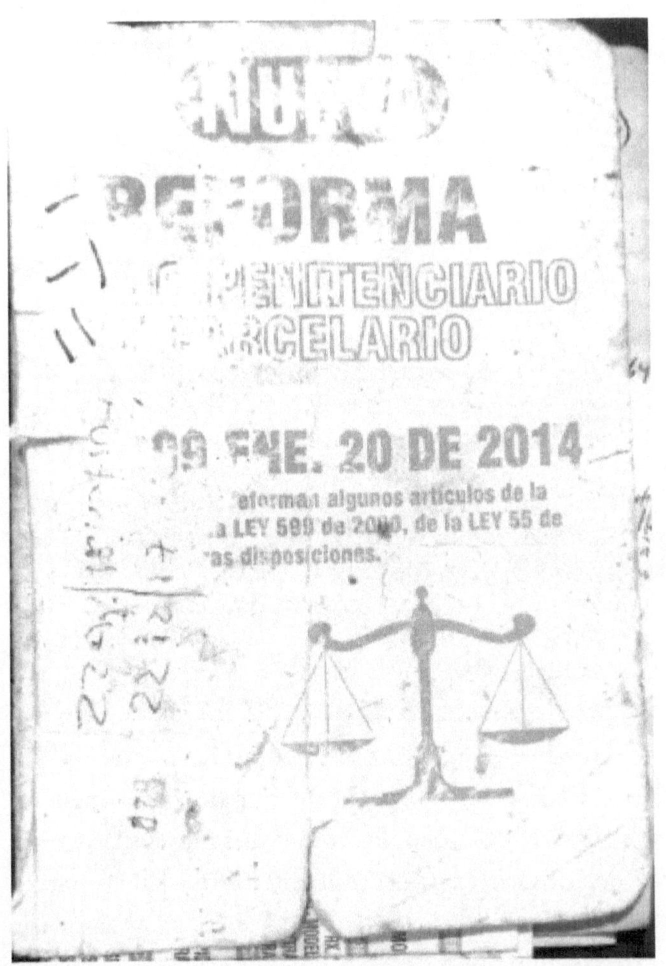


*Aristides prison handbook*

# Chapter 4: My brother from another mother



Now that Alex is on patio seven, Blake is the only person left in our prison alliance. Blake is only 32 years old, but as I mentioned, we look enough alike that the people around us assume that we are siblings. We decided early on, just moments after we met that we were pretend to be siblings, so we could stay together in the housing unit. We didn't know each other, but we both knew that we wouldn't survive if we didn't have someone else to look out for us.

Blake was here for drug trafficking. He would bring in drugs from Chile, after packing them around his torso under layers of sweaters, and jackets and then travel on the bus to Colombia. But that wasn't why Blake was in prison. He was in prison for not paying his back child support to an old girlfriend[13]. Blake was married and they lived just a few neighborhoods from Barrio Bachue, where I grew up. His wife was a lot older than him, in her early fifties with three grown daughters. They had only been married for two years when he was sentenced. His wife made a lot of sacrifices to be with Blake on visiting days, and to bring him food. They lived far from the prison and had to leave in the middle of the night to get in the visitors' queue. They didn't have a lot of money, so they would have to take Transmileno and then trudge from the station, down a dark stretch to the prison campus.

His wife and her daughters would wait hours and hours in the cold, damp night air outside the prison on visiting days to wait in the long lines to bring in homemade fajitas and tortillas[14]. Depending on the whims of the guards, the food would be inspected, searched and then either approved for entry or thrown into a huge trash bin near the entry gate. Some of the guards seemed to take great pleasure in throwing out these homemade treats.

Blake had an uncontrollable addiction to marijuana. He would smoke all day, every day to maintain his high. Even before coming to La Picota, marijuana ruled his life. He would sell his personal possessions to make sure he had enough marijuana. It made me sad to see that Blake never ate any of the food that his family brought with some much effort. He would always sell the food to get more weed.

Blake was one of the few people to be released due to the pandemic. Unlike Iran and other countries that released large numbers of incarcerated people during the pandemic to limit the spread of Covid – 19, Colombia only released a select group of people[15]. The Colombian justice minister initially announced that a small number of inmates would be released, but this was only in response to a large prison riot at La Modelo that resulted in the deaths of 23 inmates. I am glad that at least Blake got out, even if the rest of us had to stay here like sitting ducks waiting for some unknown, mystery disease to strike.

# Chapter 5: Covid 19 and Patio Six

Even now, it's kind of hard for me to wrap my mind around the fact that the whole world was locked down because of Covid while I was in prison. My family and Monica kept trying to explain it to me, but it didn't really register until I got out and looked around. That's when I noticed that every person, I saw seemed fatter than before[16]. Even after that, it is still difficult to believe that while I was locked in my cell, so was the rest of the world.

The initial outbreak of Covid was terrifying for many reasons. The prison is so crowded, that we are right on top of each other. We have so little basic hygiene. Most of the time, we don't even have clean water. The idea of an airborne infectious disease that kills people is frightening, especially because it seems like no one out there even cares. It's like because we've been convicted of a crime, everyone out there thinks that it's okay if it turns into a death sentence due to disease, malnutrition or just plain old neglect. Infection for people in our circumstances wasn't avoidable, it was inevitable[17].

*Prison overcrowding, Bogota. Photo courtesy of*
*http://misionerosporprisioneros.yolasite.com/*

At the beginning of the pandemic, we tried to protest these conditions. All of the logical and reasonable-sounded advice of the medical experts was being ignored. It seemed like the government and prison officials wanted us to get it. Maybe they figured if enough of us got sick, it would solve their overcrowding problem. They took so few precautions. They transferred infected prisoners here and there, guards were coming and going all the time, and there was no effort to separate the sick from the well. As we watched the predictable development of cases within the prison system, we decided to protest. The protests at La Modelo turned violent, but our protests here were tame. In patio six, we made signs and displayed them. Even after all the deaths during the riots at La Modelo attracted international attention, and calls for early release, the prison officials just ignored it[18]. It's astounding to me that Turkey, Iran, the Philippines, Iraq and Ethiopia released large numbers of inmates to prevent the spread of Covid, but Colombia and other democratic countries didn't[19]. I know that North Americans usually consider Colombia to be a backwards, drug-riddled narco state, (especially ones that haven't been here), but that's not actually the case. For the most part, despite being wrongfully incarcerated, I love my country and I am proud to be Colombian. My country has its problems, and a widely publicized troubled past, but it's a beautiful progressive country. In a lot of ways, Colombia is a lot more progressive that the United States. We have better nutrition, a higher standard of living, and a better healthcare system, for example. So, it's disturbing and distressing to think that repressive places like Iran and Iraq showed more compassion than my own country did. Maybe they didn't do it for wholly altruistic reasons, but they did it all the same.

While I didn't get really sick with Covid, several people on Patio 6 did. Four people here had to go to the intensive care unit. Several people on the other patios died. We wore cloth masks in our cells but it was a joke; given how crowded it was.

In July of 2021 they came to the prison and vaccinated us with the Johnson & Johnson vaccine. Most of the country had already been offered the vaccine, but I was surprised we got it at all. I mean, we can't get clean water and fresh food, so why would we be offered a lifesaving vaccine?

When (Marnie) told me that around the same time in the United States, the majority of inmates had been vaccinated, but the prison guards hadn't because they had refused the vaccine, I was incredulous[20]. It seems so unbelievably stupid. At La Picota, the guards queued up quickly for the vaccine, even more so after a guard who was on vacation caught Covid and died.

While I was here, it seems like the whole world was dying. My favorite maternal aunt lost three members of her family in just a matter of weeks. All the news from the outside was dismal. Covid appeared to be raging unstoppable across the globe. The news showed piles of bodies in the streets in Ecuador and funeral pyres in India that could be seen from space. The business districts in some of the world's largest cities were empty. Whole cities in China were ghost towns, as residents were forced to stay in their homes. Stacks of coffins and newly turned graves extending out into the Amazon jungle in Brazil, and refrigerated trucks in New York City. Everywhere there were doctors and nurses on television, crying.

But none of that was real to me. In La Picota, the worst part about Covid 19 was all of the visitation restrictions. While it made sense, it made a terrible situation even more frightening and isolating. I didn't get to see any of my family members for two years.

Before the Covid-19 pandemic began, inmates could receive visitors every weekend. Male visitors could come on Saturdays, and my dad visited me every single Saturday after my incarceration, even though it meant he had to come from his house in Sopo, which is about an hour away from the northern edge of Bogota[21]. My mom, my sister and my uncles would visit. Many of my close friends came by and saw me. Diana even remained decent to the point where she allowed my daughter Sara to come for a visit once before she moved them both to Cali [22]. Yajaira only visited once after I entered La Picota, but then she never came again. She had assumed the day-to-day care of her elderly parents back here in Bogota after her favorite uncle died. She had already had to deal with Diana firsthand during our relationship, and Diana's attempts to manipulate, control and sabotage our relationship. I think that now having a boyfriend in prison, waiting in the dark in a long line with all the other women for hours just to see me for an afternoon, was just too much for our relationship. We parted on good terms, but it was another blow to lose my lovely Angel, who had brought me back to life.

Our lives shrank after Covid, now that family visits were restricted. We no longer had news from home or contact with our family. We no longer received the delicious meals from home, that sustained us. We no longer received the stolen afternoons of intimate affection, and the love that kept us connected to the outside world. We need believe that other people love us, believe in us and wait for us. Without that, we lose our humanity. We become the soulless criminals that they accuse us of being. When there is no one who cares for you, you risk becoming a callous person who disregards the feelings of other people. My only sliver of family connection that remained were the rare care packages and letters, and our principal lifeline, the clandestine cellphone.

Clandestine cellphones aren't really clandestine. They are bought and paid for with almost daily bribes to the guards. They know we have them, and they do almost nothing to stop us. They would rather receive the regular bribes that supplement their meager salaries[23]. Given their appallingly low wages as public safety officers and dangerous and difficult work conditions, it's no surprise that many of the guards look the other way, as long as the money keeps coming. Of course, after every majority security incident or patio infraction, the guards get together to search cells, and confiscate our cell phones and other contraband.

I usually had a cell phone, sometimes my own, and sometimes a cell phone that I rented from other inmates. Sometimes after a patio sweep, or another demand for money from the guards, I would get so frustrated that I would give up on having my own cell phone. But then, I would break down because it was the only way that I could stay in contact with my daughter, my mother and Monica.

My mother and Monica had stayed in contact with each other for years, after Monica and I broke up in 2016. Monica would meet my mother for lunch every so often, and they had an active Facebook connection. Monica had been working outside of Bogota, but during her periodic returns to the city, she would always seek out my mom. Surprisingly, I was not usually the topic of conversation, until my unfortunate incarceration. Instead, they would talk about work, fashion, travel or just about anything else. They had always gotten along, especially after I'd taken Monica to play tejo with my mom one Sunday[24]. My mom had been a local tejo champion, so she had been the perfect person to introduce Monica to the game.

Monica was from France, but she had a huge enthusiasm for just about anything Colombian culture related, so she loved tejo. We spent a lovely afternoon outside Bogota, playing tejo and drinking beer, and Monica developed a friendship with my mother.

Now as she conversed with my mother, via Facebook while she was working back in France, or over coffee during her visits back to Bogota, my mother gave her my latest contact information. She sent me a tentative text, like she wasn't sure I'd respond. Maybe if I'd been in a different circumstance, I wouldn't have. After my episode of acute hepatitis, we'd had infrequent contact via Facebook before I'd been captured.

But I was alone, and lonely. I'd forgiven Monica a long time ago – and now she was reaching out, yet again, and offering a lifeline. I took it. It was difficult sometimes, Monica's Spanish is not good, and my French is non-existent, but we work at it, every day. We've had our disagreements and misunderstandings, but neither of us are the yelling, screaming, carrying on kind of people. After one big disagreement, that meant we didn't talk for a whole day, it turned out that it was all a misunderstanding due to a mistranslation between Monica, myself and google translate. But it was a rough day in La Picota that day, feeling like I'd lost something.

After that, we instituted an informal policy where no disagreement is a real disagreement unless we are certain that the other person understands exactly what we are saying. There is so much nuance within a language, that it's easy to miss subtext or subtleties. People always say that French and Spanish are so much alike, and they are, until they aren't. Even now that I am out, we still adhere to the policy. I check with Monica during our conversations, especially if she's tired or stressed, because that's when her understanding of Spanish seems to deteriorate. She definitely speaks better than she comprehends when someone else talks. Her grammar is a mess, but I don't care. I can always tell that she is sincere, which is a change from my other relationships. While I was in La Picota, I tried to remain in contact with her every day. When she was here in Bogota, I could call her on the payphones on the patio too.

Later, when they finally began allowing occasional visits again, Monica was out there in the cold mountain air, at 3 am with the other women, waiting in line for the prison gates to open at 8 am. She went thru the various lines, checks and pat downs to come see me for a few hours.

It was harder when she was back in France, due to the time differences and her schedule. She's a freelance photographer, so she worked all kinds of hours to get the photos she needs to sell to different magazines. But we would still manage to find a few minutes no matter what to exchange texts and talk to each other. I don't know if I love her, but I don't know if I can love another woman in my life. After La Picota, and the woman who put me there, I just don't know if I can care about someone in that way again. But she likes to fuss over me, and take care of me, so I let her. It's better than being alone. She makes a lot of plans for a shared future together, and I go along with it. It doesn't hurt anything and it saves me from having to have the kind of conversations that don't often end well. She's not a bad person, and it would hurt her to know what I really feel, or don't feel for her. I know I will have to have the conversation with her one day, but not today. We get along well most of the time, I make her happy, and I am still on house arrest at my mom's house so it's not like any decisions have to be made right now. I am still technically married to the Chilean woman that put me in prison in the first place, and that's a good excuse as to why I can't commit to anything more formal with her. I know that one day it's going to blow up in my face, but I'll face it when it happens.

# Chapter 6: Life on the Patio

Prison, like everything else in life, has its own routine. You don't want to admit it, but you also need that routine. No one wants to acknowledge, at least to themselves, that they have gotten used to prison, or that they have settled in to being an inmate. But that's exactly what happens. The routine of the prison gradually becomes more and more familiar, until its automatic like brushing your teeth. You don't think about the motions after a while, you just pass through the days. But then, there are days, when that rhythm is off, and you can just feel it. After a couple of times, you start to see the signs that you could only feel before. The patio is more subdued, with the guards on edge. They feel it too. Sometimes, I think even just this feeling can spark something that might not have otherwise happened, making it a bit of a self-fulfilling prophesy. Nerves are on edge and tempers flare making small arguments, or sideways glances turn into violent altercations.

Other times, inmates lash out for real world hurts and insults. Physical fights were frequent on patio six, happening just about every day, but there were few fatalities. It wasn't like some of the other patios or La Modelo prison, where fights were assassination attempts disguised as routine altercations.

One of the more memorable fights that I witnessed happened on Easter Friday. There was a tall black inmate named Betz who was scheduled to be released in three months, when he got in a fight with a small, thin white guy in his forties. Betz had gotten sexually involved with the other inmate's wife. It all started oddly enough during a conjugal visit between the other inmate and his wife. She went to the toilet to clean up after having sex with her husband. That's when she met Betz outside the bathroom stall. Rumor has it that she was immediately enthralled and transferred her affections to Betz. Rumor or not, before long the other's inmate's wife was coming to the prison for conjugal visits with Betz, not her husband – and her husband was none too pleased about it. Betz won the fight, and the wife but caused several severe facial fractures to the other inmate in the process. For this, he was received seven more years on his sentence.

I often rented tents to Betz on Sundays. He seemed to have a variety of women that visited him. I suspected that he had a bunch of mules bringing in drugs, but now I wonder if he was renting the tents to use with the other man's wife. Of course, it didn't matter anyway, because its none of my business. I got along okay with Betz, because we were basically indifferent to each other. He would sometimes try to get me to extend him credit for motel rental, but I never extend credit to anyone, doesn't matter who they are. I don't do favors for people either.

Business is one thing, and friendship is another. There were a lot of sad stories on the patio, but I didn't know many of them – which suited me fine. No one's story in this place is a happy one, and I think it's emotionally numbing to see so much misery every day.

I worry that being here, around such dysfunction, tragedy and wasted lives will change me forever. I still want to be the joyful optimist that I was before I came here. People always told me that I was laughing and smiling all the time and cheering them up with my silly jokes. I don't feel like laughing much these days, and any joy or optimism I had seems to have gone on sabbatical. I don't know if it will come back now that I have seen and experienced what I've seen. I'd like to ask some of the other inmates about it, but I can't think of anyone on the patio that I'd want to talk about this with. I wonder if this is how people who survived concentration camps and the holocaust felt. I remember reading about Anne Franks' father, Otto Frank, who was the sole member of the Attic and the Frank family to survive the death camps. He eventually remarried, to another camp survivor, and they dedicated their lives to keeping his daughter, Anne's diary in print. Did he ever laugh with his new wife? Did they ever do any silly just for fun? Did he ever just feel the pure joy that comes with being in the company of people you love? Or was that all taken from him? I want to feel that burst of joy, happiness and love that I always have when I look at my daughter. I want to be able to take pleasure in all the usual things I enjoy; traveling the countryside to see different towns, cities and nature parks. I want that sense of satisfaction when I look into my camera and see that I have the perfect shot. I want to feel desire from having my lover stoke my face and she tells me how she loves me. Don't let that be gone. Sometimes, I think it just might be, and that makes me incredibly sad, and angry at the same. It's bad enough that I went to prison. It's something that will follow me for the rest of my life. There are a lot of things I will never be able to do now. I am permanently tattooed as a criminal for the rest of my life. But it doesn't seem right that I am losing so much more from my life, and how prison has changed me, even as I do everything I can to try and prevent this. I want to be able to laugh, and to love. I want to be able to be happy again. Don't let Andrea, La Picota and the Colombian justice system take those things from me.

Don't get me wrong. I know that I am not in a death camp, where people are forcibly trying to exterminate me. La Picota is not part of the "Final Solution," per se, but the crowded conditions, inadequate food and unhygienic conditions sure make the think that the government might not be *that* opposed to the idea.

I don't know why locking me up way from my family in a tiny, shared cell isn't enough. Why do we have to be in fear for our safety all of the time? Why do they allow all of the corruption and rot to pervade the entire system – where the inmates of Patio Six are served rotting and moldy food while the politicians and other public figures get catered meals? Many of these people are mass murderers, by either tactic agreement with narcotraffickers or through the machinations of their malfeasance. But they travel in and out of La Picota in a revolving door, no matter what they do. The guards are helpful, respectful and kind servants to this group of convicted criminals. But not the rest of us, even in Patio Six, where life is better than it could be. But why do we have to be degraded day after day, until all dignity and hope is destroyed? Sometimes I feel that I am just a shell of a man.

# Chapter 7: Life after incarceration

Now that I am out, life just doesn't go back to the way it was before my arrest. For one thing, I am confined to my mother's apartment, and that can be a little too cozy sometimes. I am 47 years old, and I was sleeping on a couch in my mother's living room at first, because she had rented out my room.

Monica had found a small little house for the two of us in the northern part of the city, and she was anxiously awaiting for me to be able to come and live there with her. But due to the restrictions and requirements for me to be released early, onto house arrest, I had to go to my mother's house. Her neighbors had to vouch for my character before the judge would let me out. Some of her neighbors have known me since I was a tiny boy.

Since Monica moved to the new place while I was in here, there were no neighbors to attest to my upstanding citizenry. But she's here in Colombia, so we are trying to navigate the new dynamics. She finally got her visa after a long drawn-out process that was complicated by the pandemic. That's actually where she met the girl that led to this book. They were next to each other at the Office of Extranjeros where they issue visas. After standing in line by each other for several hours, Monica and the other girl became friendly towards each other. The other girl was a gringo too, and so they chatted while they waited, and found out that they have a couple friends in common. When they realized that they lived in the same barrio, they decided to stop for coffee before taking the bus home together on the way back to celebrate their visas.

But everything isn't hunky dory with Monica either. I don't know if it was the pandemic, or me being locked up, or maybe even me being locked up during a global pandemic, but Monica isn't the same person she was when all of this started. She was such a strong confident person when this all started, and she's not anymore. It's like she's been broken down by sadness and tragedy. I know that she had some losses due to Covid, and I know she was endlessly worried about me getting sick, but I didn't realize how hard it hit her until very recently. She's not the person I fell in love with those many years ago. She's like a broken version of that person; insecure and frightened by shadows. She wakes up gasping and shaking in the middle of the night, when she sleeps at all. Otherwise, she's restless; tossing and turning when she stays the night in my tiny space and my twin bed. She's needy and clingy where she was independent and proud before. I was proud of her independence before, it made her different from the other women I had been with. She was strong, she was self-confident, she didn't need me, and if I didn't like it, she didn't give a damn. I liked that Monica an awful lot.

Now she has these terrible periods of depression, where she just starts crying uncontrollably. She even tells me, "I don't know why I am crying," but the tears keep coming. She says it's post-traumatic stress disorder but whatever it is, it isn't normal. I feel like La Picota broke her, and I don't know if I will ever get my old, carefree, confident and happy Monica back. She has a lot of plans for our future, which makes me hopeful that she'll get better, but everything is still on hold while I remain on house arrest. It's probably better that way, because I as I mentioned before, at some point, I am going to have to have some difficult conversations with her.

My application to come off of what they call 'conditional release' or house arrest is denied, after the judge decides that I should have paid restitution to Andrea. It seems unfair to me to be punishing me for not paying something that I was never ordered to pay. It also seems like I am being set up to fail, since the judge never specified how much restitution she wants me to pay when she denies my application. It also seems calculated to keep me on house arrest almost indefinitely. I've managed to find some work through friends, but steady employment is difficult to come by for someone with a criminal record. It's even harder when you can't leave your house. I guess in that respect, Covid has done me some favors. A few years ago, the part-time job I am doing now would require me to work at a call center. Now that people have been working from home for the last few years, it's no big deal for me to do the same. It pays me a marginal amount, which I have been using to try and catch up on all the back child support I accrued while I was in prison. I don't want to get sent back to prison for that. I also want to support my daughter. She's mine and I love her. I already lost some much time in her life, and I don't want to do anything that means I won't be able to see her grow up. She needs her dad. She has a stepdad in Cali, and he seems to be a pretty decent fellow, (and a stabilizing influence on Diana) but she still needs her dad. Besides, even though Diana just got married, I already hear her arguing and bickering with her new husband in the background when I call my daughter. So now I am going to write another petition to the judge and suggest an amount for reparations. It makes me physically ill to think of giving Andrea any money after what she's done, but I can't let this be the roadblock that keeps me from living my life. Instead, I need to figure out how to pay it, so I can move on. I am pretty sure Monica would pay it for me, but that's just not something I would ever ask for.

I sometimes wonder how Andrea can live with herself, knowing that she set me up. She knows I never hurt her. She could have backed down at any time, but she followed through and made sure I was punished. I think she did it more to punish me for not being the husband she wanted that anything else. I sometimes wonder what happened with her and her powerful lover, but then I get so angry at what happened to me, that I have to think about something else. I like to think that there's karma out there somewhere, but so far, I've seen no evidence of that. For all I know, she has married someone else, and is being chauffeured around like the Queen of Sheba, living the life she always coveted, without remorse. That's probably closer to the truth than anything else.

# Chapter 8: Monica



*Author's note: At the conclusion of my series of interviews with Aristides, I conducted two lengthy interviews with Monica. I thought it was important to include her thoughts on this experience.*

I wonder sometimes if I built myself this fairytale fantasy about Aristides' return. We had originally broken up on such a bittersweet note. Or rather, I had broken up with him all those years ago, when I was being recalled to the United States. At the time I thought it wasn't fair to offer him a long-distance relationship when I didn't know if or when I'd ever be able to return to Colombia. I've always considered myself a pragmatic, logical person but maybe I just wanted to think I was. This whole experience has made me question who I really am. But at the time, the logical, rational part of me said long distance relationships don't work, and that it was unfair to expect Aristides to wait for me. I had adored him unequivocally and completely since we had started dating, in a deep and profound way that I hadn't felt for anyone else. But maybe I broke up with him because deep down inside I knew it would hurt if he left me, or if he ended up cheating on me. I can do a whole monologue about how many of my countrymen (and women) have embraced polyamory or non monogamous relationships, and even argue in a logical fashion that this lifestyle makes sense, but deep down, I just know it would hurt to find out that Aristides wanted to be with, or decided to be with someone else. So may now, all these years later, I can admit that these feelings and fears probably played a role in my decision-making. Maybe if I hadn't had been forced to return home, our romance would have run its course, but I did go home, and we did break up. Aristides remained on the forefront of my mind for a very long time after that. Even after I had moved on to another relationship, he remained in my mind. Part of me, that logical part, says that I just romanticized it all after the fact, but there is another part of me, the part that has all those sweet memories of the early halcyon days of our romance. That previously hidden, private romantic me yearned for him.

When he went to prison, I mourned. Later, when I returned to Bogota, I couldn't forget it. It was like every corner of the city held his scent, or a glimmer of memory. I met with his mother several times, and this only sharpened my yearning.

I began writing him while he was in prison. Long, lengthy texts along with a notebook of letters that I never sent. I told him about my dreams, my current work and life and I told him how I missed him. I began to include him in my dreams and plans for the future. At first, I did it to help him fight the despair and hopelessness that I could feel in him. Then later, I came to believe that those fanciful dreams could come true. That we could reunite and make a life together. That we could erase the pain of La Picota together, or at least copy over it, like we used to do with old VHS videotapes. But that's not how life works. A lot of things happened while he was in prison, much of which I don't know anything about. He won't talk to me about any of it and seems increasingly resentful when I ask. When I first asked him about speaking with you, and doing this project, I thought it would be cathartic for him. He seemed to want to do it – or at least, that's what he expressed to me. But now he's increasingly resentful and angry if I ask anything. I think he feels like I forced him to do this. I feel sorry for that. But I feel sorry for a lot of things now.

We have been through so much, collectively and individually. He had to be *there*, and I know that none of my experiences can ever be compared. But at the same time, while he was locked up, billions of us were locked down. I had multiple friends die, along with several co-workers, of a strange and terrible disease that seemed to callously pick and chose who to maim and who to kill at almost random. While two of my colleagues were older, and close to retirement age, my friends weren't. They were young and healthy until the day they weren't. Then they died. The first one of my friends to die was a marathon runner, for Christ's sake. He seemed to be recovering, and then he was dead. Another friend was joyously awaiting the last months of a joyous pregnancy, then she was in the intensive care unit, then she was intubated and then she, and what would have been her baby girl, were buried almost before any of her friends knew she had died. I think that traumatized me as well, this feeling of being caged away from my loved ones while these terrible things were happening. I can't stop wondering if my friends died alone. You would think that this shared sense of isolation would have brought Aristides and I together, and maybe, at first it did.

When he was first released onto house arrest, he didn't even tell me. He had mentioned that he had petitioned the judge, and that he would be released, but at that point, he didn't have a release date. Then I stopped hearing from him. Sometimes that happened when the guards raided the cells for contraband, and then a few days later, I would get a message. But the days passed, and then a week. I tried not to worry, but that's impossible.

I only found out he was out, when I panicked and contacted his mom to see if she had heard any news of him. She texted me back a photo of all of them sitting together, and then handed him the phone. He's never mentioned anything about this to me. I try to tell myself that maybe it all happened so fast, that he didn't have time to tell me. I tell myself that he was in the midst of being reunited with his family, so he was too busy to contact me. But really, I just remember the hurt of being so worried that something had happened, that he'd been attacked or injured. Or that maybe he had fallen ill. Only to find out, that he never even attempted to send me a short message to say, 'Hey, I am being released on this date.' That hurt has never really gone away, and I guess it's part of the reason I have started to second guess myself and the relationship. How long would it have taken him to contact me and let me know he was just across town? If I hadn't texted, would he have ever contacted me? These sorts of things go through my mind, even when things were good.

Now that the immediate joy of his release has settled, and we've moved into what seems like an eternal wait for him to be able to leave the threshold of his mother's house, it plagues me more and more. When he first came home, he always affectionate, and loving. It seemed like despite all the pain, and the obstacles, that we could have a happy ending. Or a happy something. But then, after wanting me at his side all the time, he decided that I needed to be a secret from his daughter and his ex. I understood that he didn't want any extra problems from Diana, but when his daughter came to stay for three weeks, I didn't see him for three weeks, even though he was just across the city. Even now, when she calls, he pretends I am not there. He makes sure she can't see me, and that's what I remain; a small, invisible part of his life.

He tells me he loves me, almost by rote – like a call and response, but it's what he doesn't say that haunts me. It's hard to explain to someone when he's always helping me with small things that I still struggle with in Spanish, that it hurts that he doesn't ever tell me I'm pretty, or smart or any of the thousand things I am often saying to him. Part of me says that I am being stupid and unreasonable; after all, I'm not pretty and I've gained weight since he's been away. But I haven't lost my intellect, which he used to seem to enjoy. That same part of me chides me for being selfish. Here he is, taking time to help me whenever I ask, and I'm questioning his devotion, the voice says.

But that doesn't drown out that niggling feeling that I have. The feeling that comes from the fact that even when I am gone for several days, he doesn't seem anxious or even eager to embrace me. That observation that I am the only one to ever initiate affection. That on the short weekend at his house, he gets visibly frustrated at me, several times. That he gets so angry and frustrated with me, when I am trying to snuggle close to him at night, that he flees the tiny bed to sleep on the even tinier couch in the living room. I find myself trying to buy his affection with gifts and more gifts, as if that will somehow make him love me. I am devastated when during one stupid, quick argument that erupted, he cuts me off, cuts me to pieces with his words and then flees. During one such argument, he tells me that "You aren't a parent, so you don't know anything." It cuts me, and wounds me deeply to know that he sees me in such black and white terms.

I think I know where this relationship is headed, even if I couldn't admit to myself until I started talking to you, but I am just not ready to give up yet. I am not sure what that says about me. That I am a fool? I certainly feel like one, to be chasing after a dream that no longer exists. To set myself up for loneliness and rejection over and over, as he turns away from me, again and again. Is this part of the price we have to pay for his incarceration? Or was it always destined to be this way, and I was just deceiving myself? Sometimes it's hard for me to look myself in the mirror anymore. I don't like the person I see there. The stupid middle-aged woman who is so needy that she stays, even feeling this way? Such a stupid, stupid woman, who keeps trying to see the "bright side" in his actions instead of the obvious truths. What happened to the brave, intrepid, independent woman, the one that first set out for South America, to blaze her own path, to make her own way. The woman who refused to look back, and only looked forward. The woman who believed that regrets were a waste of time and had an intrinsic sense of self-worth? Or did she flee with her dignity, the first time the cell doors swung shut?"

Finally finished with her monologue and emotionally overwrought, Monica is devastated and completely exhausted. Tears track down her face unchecked as she blows her nose.

*Marnie notes that* Monica doesn't say anything as I finish my notes. The silent is powerful in the small space as my pen glides across the notebook. I can hear the tick-tick of the kitchen clock, the occasional sniffles, a deep sigh. Outside, I can hear the noise of the city from the street near the window. Horns blare, gears grind, and motorcycle engines whine thru the air. Scattered shouts, and laughter outside contrast with the stillness and quiet gloom of the apartment. Finally, I finish my last notes, and look up at Monica.

"Did the prison do this?" I ask her.

Monica takes a stuttering inhale, wipes her eyes, and nods, saying, "I'd like to think that's what it is. I think that all the years of waiting in his cell have destroyed his patience. Most of our problems seem to stem from his impatience."

I am not sure what she means by that, and so I ask her to explain.

"When we met, I was thin, blonde and young, but I didn't speak much Spanish. But it didn't matter because Aristides was always so patient with me. He didn't mind if he had to explain something to me several times to make me understand. He didn't mind waiting while I looked things up in my old-fashioned pocket dictionary. Now, all of that is gone. He can't even be bothered to wait for me to translate something on my phone before he starts sighing and rolling his eyes at me. If I don't understand immediately, he becomes so angry, and so frustrated at me." Her eyes look so sad as she talks to me, and more tears slip down her cheeks.

"We have fallen into the horrible cycle; he gets frustrated at me, I cry, then he storms off and I just want to die," Monica continues. She looks directly at me.

"I know you don't know me, but that's not who I am, that's not who I was," she states.

*Marnie:* Her pain, and sadness are uncomfortable in the small stuffy apartment. It's a surprise to me, that I feel this way, in her presence. I've interviewed grieving widows across the globe, in war-torn country. I've spoke to mothers as they held their dead and dying children. I've photographed and spoke to refugees as they search thru the rubble of crowded shelters for some remainder of their tattered belongings, a photo, a favorite shirt, a child's toy. I'd grown familiar with loss, and even more so after my husband's murder. I worried that I'd become callous over the years, but now I can't even stand to be in the presence of this sad, suffering woman. I touch her hand softly, as I thank her and take my leave. Later as I put her words to these pages, her pain gnaws at me.

I contemplate this as I pack my meager belongings to return to my life in Memphis. It's time to wrap this project up. I've already been gone much longer than I ever anticipated. Her sorrow stays with me, haunts me. It takes me back to those dark, bleak days after Ahmad died. That awareness snaps me back to the present, and I feel suddenly angry. When I acknowledge that it's anger that I am feeling; I realize that I have gotten in too deep, too close to the story. I am no longer just an observer, taking notes. I am taken aback by this. It's not part of Aristides story. But I can't stop being angry, and I have to resolve this. I have to talk to Aristides again.

# Chapter Nine: Aristides

═══

We meet again, this time at a coffee shop in the shopping center by my house. I am tired, after working a long shift at the thankless job that is part of my conditional release. My boss knows it, and takes advantage of it, not even paying me the minimum wage I am entitled to. I wonder what sort of thoughts go thru the minds of people like this – people willing to turn ex-cons like me into indentured slaves.

I am surprised to see that the writer looks as tired as I do. I don't think of writing as job, really, so I am shocked to see her looking as if she's spent all day hauling boxes. Her hair is mussed, her clothing is wrinkled, and she looks mildly sweaty despite the cool breeze in the air.

She surprises me again, but foregoing any polite formalities, or small talk. I have heard that North Americans are more abrupt, but I hadn't seen it before on the other occasions when we talked. Monica is never abrupt, she's always patient, even slow at times. Marnie says that she's heading back home to the United States and needs to ask some more questions and review some of her notes, so she can finish the book once she gets home. I offer my email, but she shrugs it away, casually.

I sip hot chocolate, slowly as she pulls out her pen and a battered notebook. She explains that she has been to see Monica recently.

"Aristides, do you love her?" she asks point-blank. I keep my face neutral, but I feel a flash of annoyance. I wonder if she has been enlisted by Monica to try and make me feel guilty. I won't be played, I won't be manipulated, and I certainly won't be controlled, by any woman.

I also feel annoyed that this woman is asking me this. Didn't I explain myself before? I know she heard me last time we talked, I mean, she even took notes. I talk another sip of my hot chocolate, while she waits for me to respond, her face earnest. There is something else in her face, that I can't quite identify. Something bitter, that I hadn't detected before.

Marnie waits, but when I don't answer, she finally says, "If you don't love her, or don't value her, just leave. It's not fair of you to stay. That takes away her opportunity to find someone who really loves her."

Marnie continues, "You know, situations like this really just piss me off. Two people just messing things up. Some of us never even get the opportunity to love someone long enough to mess things up."

"Stop being so fucking selfish!" she finally says to me, before abruptly standing up and walking away.

She leaves, and we never talk in person again. She sends me several formal emails with additional questions to answer, and asks me to write a couple more chapters in my own words, to be translated later, including this one. She wanted to know how my story ended, but it doesn't end, does it?

# PostScript: Marnie

I WAS EDITING THIS project in the Summer of 2024 when I decided to reach out to Monica and Aristides again, to see how they were. The book had been horribly delayed so part of the reason I was contacting the couple was to apologize. However, when I spoke with Monica, she explained that she and Aristides were no longer together. He had left her for a younger woman. He had also recently been diagnosed with stomach cancer. She didn't give me all of the details because she was too overcome with grief. I tried to contact Aristides several times, but he never returned any of my numerous messages. I wish I had a better ending for readers, but it seems like there are very few happy endings for people who go to prison, even under the best of circumstances.

# Reference notes and further recommended reading

1. LITERAL TRANSLATIONS may vary but the regional use of the verb 'culiar' in Bogota and Colombia in general is a very crude term for sex, akin to "fuck".

2. (2016, February 17). Scores of dismembered bodies found in Colombian jails. *Reuters.* Accessed at https://www.reuters.com/article/us-colombia-crime-idUSKCN0VQ2IP

(2016, February 18). Colombia probes disappears from Bogota prison. *BBC news.* Accessed at https://www.bbc.com/news/world-latin-america-35603022

(2020, March 20). Fire in La Picota prison in Bogotá reveals humanitarian emergency. *Colombia Informa.com* Accessed at https://www.colombiainforma.info/incendio-en-carcel-la-picota-de-bogota-revela-emergencia-humanitaria/

3. (2019, November 19). More than half of the people convicted for corruption receive house arrest. *El Tiempo.* Accessed at https://www.eltiempo.com/politica/gobierno/mas-de-la-mitad-de-condenados-por-corrupcion-en-colombia-tienen-casa-por-carcel-434802.

4. (2022, May 30). Gustavo Petro wins primary with large majority at La Picota, the same prison his brother visited. Infobae.com Accessed at https://www.infobae.com/america/colombia/2022/05/30/gustavo-petro-gano-con-amplia-mayoria-en-la-carcel-la-picota-la-misma-que-su-hermano-visito/

5. (1998, February 4). Six dead, 37 hurt in prison battle. *AP News.* Accessed at https://apnews.com/article/27d8db3100961ef50ef43f9fcb348e4c

Dayani, M. (2001). Ten die in Colombian jail violence. *UPI news.* Accessed at https://www.upi.com/Archives/2001/07/03/10-die-in-Colombia-jail-violence/2888994132800/

8. Feced, Carlos Galan (2021, May 7). Uglier than Picio, being dumber than Abundio, Bernarda, el Tato, Juan Palomo...: this is the origin of the funniest popular expressions. *Business Insider*. Accessed at https://www.businessinsider.es/feo-picio-bernarda-abundio-tato-expresiones-populares-846451

10. (2001, October 23). Colombia: Supreme court in favor of conjugal visits for lesbian inmate. *Outright International*. Accessed at https://outrightinternational.org/content/colombia-supreme-court-favor-conjugal-visits-lesbian-inmate

Duncan, Sam (2018, April 13). Cocaine Cassie's prison sex confession: Convicted drug mule, 22, opens up on 'monthly conjugal visits' from locals after confirming her split with fiance Scott Broadbridge. *Daily Mail Online*. Accessed at https://www.dailymail.co.uk/news/article-5610397/Cocaine-Cassie-Sainsbury-opens-monthly-conjugal-visits-locals-Colombian-jail.html

11. (2022 May 18). In photos: the extravagant orders that entered the pavilion of extraditables of La Picota. *RCN News*. Accessed at https://www.noticiasrcn.com/colombia/los-costosos-alimentos-que-ingresaban-a-la-carcel-la-picota-419662

Jordan, James (2010 Sept 9). The "New Penitentiary Culture": US Designs for Colombian Jails. How the USAID, Federal Bureau of Prisons and the School of the Americas Have Impacted Colombia's Prison System. *The Narco News Bulletin*. Accessed at http://narconews.com/Issue67/article4200.html

14. (2020, May 21). Defending rights of Iranian prisoners amidst the COVID-19 pandemic. *United Nations Human Rights High Commission*. Accessed at https://www.ohchr.org/en/stories/2020/05/defending-rights-iranian-prisoners-amidst-covid-19-pandemic

16. Edwards, Jessy (2020 June 4). Coronavirus hits Colombian prison population hard. Critics say the government's response to early warnings about the spread of COVID-19 in Colombian prisons was too little, too late. *Bogota Post*. Accessed at https://thebogotapost.com/coronavirus-hits-colombian-prison-population-hard/46778/

18. Beaudry G, Zhong S, Whiting D, Javid B, Frater J, Fazel S. Managing outbreaks of highly contagious diseases in prisons: a systematic review. BMJ Glob Health. 2020 Nov;5(11). Accessed at https://www.ncbi.nlm.nih.gov/pmc/articles/PMC7670855/

19. Bruce – Lockhart, Katherine (2021 November 9). More than a million prisoners have been released during COVID-19, but it's not enough. *The Conversation.* Accessed at https://theconversation.com/more-than-a-million-prisoners-have-been-released-during-covid-19-but-its-not-enough-170434

20. Worden, Amy (8 July 2021). Most incarcerated people have had their COVID-19 shots — but their guards likely haven't. *PBS Health.* Accessed at: https://www.pbs.org/newshour/health/most-incarcerated-people-have-had-their-covid-19-shots-but-their-guards-likely-havent

**Additional information:**

The UK prisoner's pack – maintained by the British government, this website holds a wealth of information for British nationals who have been arrested/ detained / incarcerated in Colombia.

https://www.gov.uk/government/publications/colombia-prisoner-pack/colombia-prisoner-pack

Wouters, Kwinten (2018, January 24). Doing time in a Colombian prison. *Bogota Post.* Accessed at https://thebogotapost.com/time-colombian-prison/26578/

*My life in La Picota, as told to Marnie Gellhorn*

[1] The inmates were yelling, "carne fresca," and "Echelo pa' culiarlo" at the new arrivals.

[2] A similar gruesome discovery was made in 2016 at Modelo Prison in Bogota.

[3] Of course, more than half of the people convicted for corruption only receive house arrest.

[4] Unsurprisingly, Gustavo Petro gained the majority of the votes cast at La Picota. (Unlike the United States, incarcerated Colombians retain the right to vote.)

[5] La Modelo is a truly horrifying place that almost defies description, where inmates have free access to guns, grenades and other weapons.

[6] The only inmates that were eligible for early release due to overcrowding were people incarcerated for nonpayment of child support. These inmates were often cycle in and out, as their financial circumstances changed.

[7] At the time of his entrance in the prison, this was about ten dollars.

[8] (2019, November 8). Bacteria en La Picota habría obligado amputaciones en dos reclusos. *El Tiempo.*

[9] Direct translation is "Uglier than horrible." The origin of this popular Colombian joke traces back to Spain, and a convoluted story about a shoemaker in Grenada in the 19th century. Nevertheless, both Chi-Chi and the unfortunate cobbler are not considered attractive by any measure.

[10] Around 150 thousand dollars at the time of his arrest.

[11] Spouse/ wife/husband can be a misnomer in Colombia. Colombia considers any period of cohabitation longer than 2 years to be a 'common-law' marriage, so Colombians commonly refer to long-term girlfriends/ boyfriends as their spouse. These conjugal visit rights have extended to same-sex couples since 2001.

[12] While the residents of R-Sur may be getting lobster and gourmet meals, the rest of La Picota is not. In fact, it has been argued by journalist James Jordan that the involvement of the US government into Colombian prison administrative has directly contributed to a decline in food quality.

[13] Nonpayment of child support makes up a considerable percentage of people incarcerated in Colombia.

[14] Prior to the pandemic, homemade food was allowed.

[15] Iran temporarily released between 80,000 to 100,000 inmates during the beginning of the pandemic.

[16] Prior to the Covid pandemic, Bogota residents were known for being slim and athletic.

[17]

[18] A study by Beaudry et al. (2020) looked at the variable responses of prison authorities in 79 countries, including Colombia to the Covid pandemic.

[19] Based on figures released by Penal Reform International.

[20] According to PBS report dated July 2021.

[21] USME, where the prison is located is on the southernmost edge of Bogota.

[22] A large city located several hours from Bogota.

[23] The average prison guard makes between 1.1 million and 2.1 million pesos per month. (Colombian minimum wage is 1 million pesos per month). Salaries are not adjusted for periodic fluctuations in currency. At the time of this writing, this is the equivalent of 275 dollars to 575 dollars a month.

[24] Tejo is the national sport, similar to horseshoes, but with the addition of small firecrackers.

# Don't miss out!

Visit the website below and you can sign up to receive emails whenever Marnie Gellhorn publishes a new book. There's no charge and no obligation.

https://books2read.com/r/B-A-YYXDC-RCGMF

**BOOKS 2 READ**

Connecting independent readers to independent writers.

# Also by Marnie Gellhorn

**Murder in the Mississippi Delta**
The Barons of Memphis
The Princes of Shelby County

**Standalone**
Three Years in a Colombian Prison: My Life in La Picota as
Told to Marnie Gellhorn

Watch for more at https://therealmarniegellhorn.com/.

# About the Author

Marnie Gellhorn is a former overseas correspondent. She has covered stories from all over the world, but most often in areas of conflict, like Syria, Iraq and Afghanistan. She has dedicated her career to putting a human face of the geopolitics of our international policies.As a frequent contributor to AP outlets, often the only byline you will have seen is Associated Press. But if you've read enough of her work, you can almost hear her soft gravelly voice in the stories.

After two decades devoted to writing about war and conflict, Marnie has begun to branch out into different area, such a s crime and justice. The Barons of Memphis is a fictionalized account of an infamous crime in for her adopted hometown. The Princes of Shelby County is a continuation of this series.

Three Years in a Colombian Prison is a non-fiction book based on interviews with a convicted inmate, Aristides Jesus Gonzalez Riohacha and his family.

Marnie and her constant companion, Henri Arthur George split their time between Memphis and Sonoma as she continues to work as a travel writer. She is a frequent contributor to wine & cheese magazine. You can find Marnie on Instagram, Facebook, Goodreads and other social media sites.

Read more at https://therealmarniegellhorn.com/.

# About the Publisher

AL Press is the independent publisher of a multitude of books by a variety of authors. While this label was started by Auguste Leon Hart; we don't specialize in any one genre, and we are always interested in adding authors to our label. We started with Auguste's whimsical vampire story, and then continued by assisting other authors in the publishing process. Not all of our affiliated titles are on-line but we have a variety of authors, genres and titles on a variety of platforms, including print medias, e-books and podcasts. We also participate (with our authors) at brick-and-mortar events; book signings, readings and book fairs.We don't have a big social media presence (though some of our authors do) because we'd rather devote our time to reviewing, editing and publishing books for readers to enjoy.

www.ingramcontent.com/pod-product-compliance
Lightning Source LLC
Chambersburg PA
CBHW031444130726
47989CB00003B/1280